J 133.3 HAM
Hamilton, John
Wizards and witches

042105

WIZARDS AND WITCHES

by John Hamilton

VISIT US AT
WWW.ABDOPUB.COM

Published by ABDO Publishing Company, 4940 Viking Drive, Suite 622, Edina, Minnesota 55435.
Copyright ©2005 by Abdo Consulting Group, Inc. International copyrights reserved in all countries.
No part of this book may be reproduced in any form without written permission from the publisher.
ABDO & Daughters™ is a trademark and logo of ABDO Publishing Company.

Printed in the United States.

Editor: Paul Joseph
Graphic Design: John Hamilton
Cover Design: TDI
Cover Illustration: *Grand Avatar,* ©1995 Don Maitz
Interior Photos and Illustrations: p 1 *Warwick's Banishment* ©1996 Don Maitz; p 5 *Grand Avatar* ©1995 Don Maitz; pp 6-7 *Riding the Storm Out* ©2002 Don Maitz; p 9 *Merlin* ©2004 Don Maitz; p 10 *Wizard's Revenge* ©1984 Don Maitz; p 11 *Visionary Wizard* ©1995 Don Maitz; p 12 Gundestrup Cauldron, Corbis; p 13 *Sorcerer's Gun* ©1999 Don Maitz; pp 14-15 *Wizard of the Owls* ©1991 Janny Wurts; p 16 Tibetan shaman, Corbis; p 17 *Greetings From The Other World* ©1979 Don Maitz; pp 18-19 *Storm Warden II* ©1994 Janny Wurts; p 20 *Wind Witch* ©1994 Don Maitz; p 21 witch, Corbis; p 22 broomstick, Corbis; p 23 *Queen of Ashes* ©1994 Don Maitz; p 24, witch dunking; Corbis; p 25 *Conjure Mice* ©1993 Don Maitz; p 26 *Sorcerer's Apprentice* ©1994 Janny Wurts; p 27 *Abracatabra* ©1994 Don Maitz; p 28 *Wizard's Touch* ©2002 Don Maitz; p 29 *Catfish* ©1996 Don Maitz; p 31 *Wizard's Dragon Crystal* ©1998 Don Maitz.

Library of Congress Cataloging-in-Publication Data

Hamilton, John, 1959–
    Wizards & witches / John Hamilton
      p. cm. — (Fantasy & folklore)
    Includes index.
    ISBN 1-59197-716-9
    1. Wizards—Juvenile literature. 2. Witches—Juvenile literature. I. Title: Wizards and witches. II. Title.

BF1589.H36 2004
133'3—dc22

                                      2004045079

CONTENTS

hocus pocus

arry Potter, the teenage wizard crafted by the imagination of author J.K. Rowling, comes from a long line of fictional magicians. For hundreds of years people have delighted in hearing the tales of Merlin, magical advisor to Britain's King Arthur. Shakespeare wrote of the magician Prospero in *The Tempest*. The last century has seen an explosion of wizard characters, from *The Wizard of Oz* to J.R.R. Tolkien's Gandalf in *The Lord of the Rings*. Mickey Mouse played a sorcerer's apprentice in Walt Disney's *Fantasia*, and of course there's Harry Potter, the promising young wizard with the lightning-shaped scar on his forehead who learns to cast spells, fight evil, and win Quidditch tournaments while riding a magical broomstick.

Wizards are an important part of literature called "high fantasy," which features knights, dragons, castles, evil lords, ladies-in-waiting, and many other elements rooted in medieval European legends and folklore. Also called sorcerers, conjurers, enchanters, mystics, and mages, wizards are mysterious characters who travel through space and time, conjure spells, transform themselves into animals, and create magic potions.

Wizards have appeared in many different ways over the centuries, but the most common image we have of them today is of gray-bearded old men wearing flowing robes and pointed hats, carrying magical staffs, usually talking in riddles or spouting advice to young adventurers, telling the future and uttering mysterious incantations in languages long dead.

Far right: Fantasy illustrator Don Maitz's *Grand Avatar.*

Wizards get their power by mastering the four basic elements—earth, fire, metal, and water. After learning to control the forces of nature, many wizards choose to use their skills to help mankind. Others become intoxicated with their newfound powers, and choose an evil path instead.

Witches, too, are an ever-present element of fantasy literature. Masters of the supernatural world, witches can practice white magic or black magic, good or bad. Broomsticks, cauldrons, potions, black cats, magic spells—these are all familiar parts of a witch's mysterious inventory. Like wizards, they conjure spells and can shape-shift into animals. Some can even control the weather.

Witches and wizards can trace their roots back thousands of years. Today, in the age of science, it's easy to think we have no more use for these mystical users of magic. But our popular culture is filled with witches riding broomsticks and wizards casting astonishing spells. In reality, the world is a complex, frightening place. We often feel powerless to control events. Perhaps we're drawn to stories of wizards and witches even today because they help us make sense of the world, giving us a fantasy in which we can control our future, and our fears.

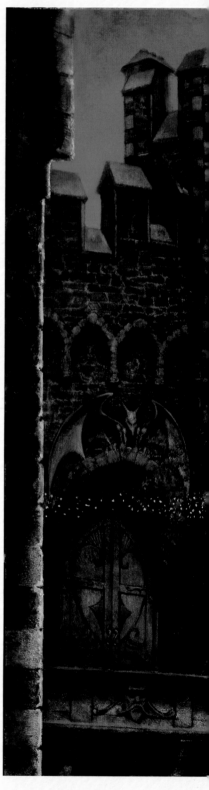

Right: Don Maitz's *Riding the Storm Out.*

Wizards in History

The adventures of Harry Potter are extremely popular today, but the teenage wizard from Hogwarts is only the latest in a long line of wizards. Before Harry Potter, there was Gandalf from *The Lord of the Rings*. Going further back in time, Shakespeare's *The Tempest* featured Prospero, the aging wizard stuck on his magical island. All these wizards are unique, but they have their roots in the one fictional wizard who is the granddaddy of them all: Merlin.

We know Merlin today mainly from Walt Disney's 1963 film, *The Sword in the Stone*, which was based on a popular 1938 book by T.H. White. In this story, Merlin is an absent-minded old magician who helps and advises young King Arthur, teaching the boy all the tools he needs to grow up and rule Great Britain. Among his many magical tricks, Merlin foretells the future, and also shows Arthur how to change himself into different kinds of animals.

In creating his story, T.H. White researched many old tales of King Arthur and Merlin, including Thomas Malory's *Morte d'Arthur*. But the person who historians think really created Merlin is a 12th-century English author called Geoffrey of Monmouth, who penned the epic *History of the Kings of Britain*. In this book, Merlin first shows up as an adviser to Vortigern, who was a 5th-century British king. Merlin also was an adviser to the next king in line, Ambrose, as well as Ambrose's brother, Uther. Uther, in turn, was the father of Arthur, future king of Britain.

Far right: Merlin, by Don Maitz.

Geoffrey of Monmouth wrote that Merlin grew to be 120 years old, perhaps explaining why in later tales he's usually described as an absent-minded old man. His mother, Geoffrey wrote, was a Welsh princess, and his father was a demon, which is how he obtained his supernatural powers. Not only could he read minds and tell the future, Geoffrey's Merlin was a large, frightening figure, of great height and strength, not at all like the wizened magician of T.H. White or Walt Disney.

Historians believe Geoffrey of Monmouth made up most of the details that come to mind today when we think of Merlin and the tales of King Arthur: the sword in the stone, the round table, Arthur's sword Excalibur, and other familiar story elements. Although the details are fiction, Geoffrey, too, was probably drawing on an historical character when he created his Merlin.

Far right: Don Maitz's *Visionary Wizard.*
Below: Wizard's Revenge, by Don Maitz.

Many think that Geoffrey of Monmouth's Merlin was possibly Myrddin, a 6th-century military leader. Myrddin went mad after witnessing six of his brothers dying in battle. Insane with grief, he fled from home and went to live alone in the woods as a wild man. He was discovered months later and brought back, but he never fully recovered his mental state. He was reported to be still half wild. He traveled with wolves and deer, and some said he could fly. He was also skilled at telling the future.

The story of Myrddin has many elements of a pre-Christian religion that dominated Britain in ancient times. The mysterious people who practiced this religion may be the ancestors of today's fictional wizards and witches. These people were the druids.

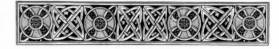

MYSTERIOUS DRUIDS

Druids were a special class of people in Celtic society, which dominated the British Isles and parts of France and Scandinavia for hundreds of years before the Roman invasion and occupation of 43 A.D. The druids were educated and literate, and were actively involved in running Celtic society. Druids included priests, judges, poets, and soothsayers. They were important because they paid attention to the cycles of nature. They preferred to hold religious ceremonies in oak groves, and used the mistletoe plant because of its healing abilities. The druids could tell their people the best time to plant crops, and when to harvest. They also claimed they could tell the future, and advised military leaders on the best times to go to war.

Far right: Sorcerer's Gun, by Don Maitz.
Below: A detail from the Gundestrup Cauldron.

Because they didn't leave behind a written record, much of what we know about druids is guesswork. Archaeological evidence helps us get a better picture of their society and practices. The Gundestrup Cauldron is a 2,000-year old solid silver pot that was unearthed from a peat bog in Denmark. It's the kind of pot you can imagine witches or wizards using to stir up batches of magical potions. Archaeologists think the cauldron was used for many years before being put in the bog as a kind of sacrifice. There are carvings on the cauldron that show horned gods and half-human, half-animal figures. There are also scenes that may depict human sacrifices.

In 1950, the mummified remains of a man were found in another Danish peat bog. The body was over 2,000 years old, yet very well preserved. Archaeologists called him Tollund Man. There is evidence that he was ritually sacrificed in a druid ceremony. His stomach contents revealed many different types of grain, which suggest a ritual last meal. Scientists also found traces of ergot, which is a toxic mold found on rye grain. Druids used ergot to induce trances and hallucinations. After his final meal, Tollund Man was strangled to death, then laid to rest in the bog. In the last 50 years, other preserved bodies have been discovered in Denmark, Germany, Ireland, and Britain.

The Romans occupied Britain for several hundred years after the invasion of 43 A.D., until about 400 A.D. During this time the Roman religion seemed to tolerate druid practices, which kept the old ways alive. The Romans didn't think much of the druids, however. They called them bloodthirsty barbarians and severely limited their political control over the people. Druids did practice human sacrifice, but many sources claim that, on the whole, the druids were actually a peaceful people who were constantly in tune with nature.

When the Roman Empire fell at the beginning of the fifth century, many people were able to revive the old druid practices, which had been handed down from generation to generation. The historical King Arthur rose at about this time in history. It makes sense that he might have had an adviser who was skilled in the old druid ways of telling the future and harnessing the forces of nature. Geoffrey of Monmouth was probably not too far off when he created his fictional Merlin.

Right: Wizard of the Owls, by fantasy illustrator Janny Wurts.

Shamans

ruids weren't the first people to try to harness the powers of magic and nature. A very ancient form of magic called shamanism existed long before the druids.

In the time before civilization, the forces of nature could be terrifying and deadly. By paying attention to the rhythms of the seasons, or knowing how particular plants could be used to heal, certain ancient people could help their tribes survive. People with this special knowledge of nature were called shamans, and they were revered as magicians. These were the earliest forms of wizards. There is archaeological evidence of shamanism reaching back 40,000 years.

Shamans were animists. They believed that animals and plants, not just human beings, have souls. They thought that the world was filled with spirits that could be communicated with, as long as one knew the proper technique.

Shamans believed that they could walk between this world and the mystical world. They did this by first going into a deep trance. The trance was achieved by either denying themselves food for a long time (fasting), or by chanting and dancing, which was often accompanied by rhythmic drumming. In many cases special medicines were given to help shamans get into the trance state.

Far right: Greetings From The Other World, by Don Maitz.
Below: A Tibetan shaman attempts to drive away evil spirits by going into a trance while beating a traditional drum.

Once a shaman was in a trance, he was able to travel to the mystical world, where he could communicate with spirits and animals. When the trance was over, the shaman then told his anxious tribemates what he had learned.

Shamans were especially valuable to ancient hunting societies. Because they were so in tune with nature and studied animal migratory routes, shamans knew where prey was likely to be found during any time of the year. It's said that shamans could also make animals appear at certain times, which must have been a valuable skill for any hunting community.

Shamans were experts with medicines. Not only did they know which medicine to use to get into a trance state, they could also concoct various medical treatments from their knowledge of plants and herbs. These medicines ranged from simple painkillers to drugs that even helped the mentally ill.

Shamanism was probably practiced in ancient societies all over the world. Evidence of their magical practice has been found as far away as Australia and the Arctic. Even today, there are some places, like Siberia and Mongolia, where shamanism is still practiced.

The ancient shaman practice of communicating with the natural world, with animals especially, can be seen in today's fictional wizards, from Merlin all the way to Harry Potter.

Right: Storm Warden II, by Janny Wurts.

Witches

fter the Roman Empire collapsed, Christianity began to take hold in Britain and the rest of Northern Europe. By about 1000 A.D. druids and their knowledge of magic were no longer tolerated. Some druids practiced in secret, but most of the old ways died out, along with the remaining few druids.

One isolated group of people—witches—kept the old traditions alive. Witches had been around for centuries, even as far back as prehistoric times. Like shamans, witches used their knowledge of the natural world to help hunters find their prey. They were also skilled at concocting spells and magic potions, and telling the future. The ancient Greeks and Romans tolerated witches in their societies. The Romans made a distinction between good magic and bad magic. Witches who practiced bad magic were punished.

Once Christianity took hold, the dividing line between good and bad sorcery was erased. All witches were considered to be worshipers of the devil. In keeping the old druid magic alive, most witches had to stay in hiding. Potions and spells were not written down out of fear of being caught. Knowledge was passed down orally from one generation of witches to the next.

Left: Wind Witch, by Don Maitz.
Far right: Actress Sigourney Weaver plays a witch in the film *Snow White: A Tale of Terror.*

Above: A witch rides on her broomstick.
Far right: Queen of Ashes, by Don Maitz.

The witches' knowledge of herbal remedies and potions became quite extensive. Many plants were boiled in large cauldrons. The cauldron is a familiar tool of witches, made famous in Shakespeare's *Macbeth*, in the scene with the three witches hovering over their boiling potion muttering, "Double, double toil and trouble. Fire burn, and cauldron bubble." Witches learned their craft after many years of practice. They had to be careful: one bad recipe could easily prove fatal.

Like the shamans and druids, witches used special medicines to help them fall into trances, which they believed allowed them to communicate with the spirit world. One of the witches' favorite trance drugs was made from mandrake, a plant of the deadly nightshade family. Their forked roots give them the resemblance of a human face. And, as if that isn't disturbing enough, folklore says that mandrakes scream when pulled from the ground. Witches used mandrakes quite often. They even make an appearance in the Harry Potter books.

When mandrakes were converted into an ointment and spread on the body, a witch went into a trance-like state, accompanied by double vision and hallucinations. One common side effect of mandrake poisoning is the sensation of flying. This might be the reason why witches today are often shown flying through the air on their broomsticks. It is a piece of folklore that probably has a root in the use of mandrakes.

As witches experimented more and more with herbs, they discovered many medicinal uses for their concoctions. Their hallucinogenic drugs may have been used as a primitive anesthesia for someone undergoing surgery. There were also many herbal remedies that acted as painkillers, or helped wounds to heal quicker. Their knowledge of medicines and natural healing was quite extensive for their time. Even today, modern pharmaceutical companies are experimenting with long-lost witches brews, including mandrakes, in the hope of discovering new treatments for diseases such as cancer.

Witches have suffered at the hands of religious authorities down through the ages. After Christianity took hold, witches were persecuted for being devil worshipers. European witch-hunts, especially in the late 1500s and 1600s, found many people falsely accused of witchcraft and devil worship. During this period of hysteria, many women were sent to prison, tortured, and executed, or banished from society. In Salem, Massachusetts, in 1692, about 150 people were imprisoned because authorities accused them of being witches. Nineteen people, men and women, were hanged. Today, most historians believe the victims were falsely accused.

During the 20th century, several writers revived an interest in witchcraft and ancient religious rituals. Modern witchcraft, often called Wicca, or the Craft, is a mix of the old ways plus elements of female, Goddess-worshiping religions and other pre-Christian beliefs.

Far right: Conjure Mice, by Don Maitz.
Below: A woman is dunked underwater during a witch trial in Salem, Massachusetts.

Scholars have trouble connecting modern witchcraft with the witches of history. Still, Wicca has a strong following today, and is considered by some to be a legitimate religion. Many are drawn to the practice because of its potential for spiritual growth, and because of its worship of the natural world. Modern witches do not practice Satanism. They insist that they create magic only for good purposes, such as love potions or healing spells. Still, many conservative religions reject Wicca's standing as a formal religion, and insist that it is a pagan practice with roots in the worship of evil powers.

Modern Wizards?

itches and wizards come from an age that seems long ago and far away. Yet, we still stand in line to buy the latest Harry Potter book, or flock to theaters to see wizards and other magical creatures in *The Lord of the Rings.* We have an unquenchable thirst for stories of fantastical sorcerers with their magic cloaks, staffs, wands, dragon scales, and magical potions. Who hasn't taken delight in the thought of riding a magical broom in the moonlight, or turning into a cat,

or telling fortunes with a shining crystal ball? It's an entertaining thought, but it's all fantasy. Then again, maybe it's not.

Some parts of the world of ancient wizards and witches can indeed be found today, if only one looks closely enough. Nobody believes people can really tell the future, yet millions read their horoscope in the daily newspaper, or consult the Tarot or I Ching.

We still celebrate Halloween, which once was a ritual, complete with animal slaughter and feasts, that ancient people conducted at the beginning of winter to summon supernatural creatures.

Left: Sorcerer's Apprentice, by Janny Wurts.
Far right: Abracatabra, by Don Maitz.

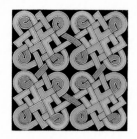

In our dance halls we can see echoes of wizards and shamans of the past. Trance dancing is a form of techno music with long periods of repetitive beats. It can bring increased creativity and mental well-being to some dancers. It is almost as if they've drifted into another reality, just as shamans did thousands of years ago.

Even in the world of science, we admire well-educated people whose knowledge of technical details is so extensive it borders on the supernatural. It's no surprise that people who are especially good with computers are often called wizards. We place our faith in these people's abilities, just as ancient societies trusted their well-being to sorcerers and witches.

Today we live in a world of high technology, where science can explain almost any mystery, or cure any ill. And yet, as long as our future is unknown, we still cling to another world, a world of wizards and magic, to help us get through our fears.

Right: Wizard's Touch, by Don Maitz.
Far right: Catfish, by Don Maitz.

GLOSSARY

ANIMISM

A belief in the existence of spirits and demons. Animists believe that all life is created by a spiritual force. They believe that all natural things, like animals, trees, or even stones, have a spirit. Animists believe that these spirits can be communicated with, if one uses the proper technique. Mystical priests called shamans were part of animist societies, and were used to talk to the spirits of the natural world.

ERGOT

A reddish-brown or black fungus that attacks certain cereal grains, especially rye. Medicines called alkaloids can be extracted from this toxic mold. Druids used ergot to bring about visions and hallucinations.

FOLKLORE

The unwritten traditions, legends, and customs of a culture. Folklore is usually passed down by word of mouth from generation to generation.

GENRE

A type, or kind, of a work of art. In literature, a genre is distinguished by a common subject, theme or style. Some genres include fantasy, science fiction, and mystery.

HALLUCINATION

The perception of a sight or sound that isn't actually there. Hallucinations can occur because of mental illness, or be induced by certain medicines. Druids and witches used medicines to bring on hallucinations in order to contact what they believed to be the spirit world.

MEDIEVAL

Something from the Middle Ages.

MIDDLE AGES

In European history, a period defined by historians as between 476 A.D. and 1450 A.D.

MISTLETOE

A parasitic evergreen plant that grows on deciduous or evergreen trees. Mistletoe has yellow-green leaves, yellow flowers, and white poisonous berries. Sprigs of mistletoe are hung at Christmas as decorations. Druids used the plant to make medicines.

MYTHOLOGY

The study or collection of myths. Myths are traditional stories collected by a culture. Their authors are almost always unknown. Myths explain the origin of mankind, or of civilizations. They also explain the customs or religions of a people. Myths are often stories that include the deeds of gods and great heroes.

NORSE

The people, language, or culture of Scandinavia, especially medieval Scandinavia.

PAGAN

Generally, a person who doesn't practice a widely recognized formal religion, such as Christianity, Judaism, or Islam. There are several definitions of the word pagan. In the context of this book, pagans are people who worship nature or the earth, such as druids or witches.

Left: Wizard's Dragon Crystal, by artist Don Maitz.

Index